365

CONNECTING
QUESTIONS

FOR COUPLES

CASEY & MEYGAN CASTON

COFOUNDERS OF MARRIAGE365

Illustration: Sel Thomson
Typesetting: Melanie Etemadi
Back Cover Photography: Andre Niesing

ISBN 978-1-7324358-0-3

Published in 2018 by Casey and Meygan Caston

To all of the people that believed in us and have given their unwavering support in our journey with Marriage365. To Kylie and Cordell and our dream that you would live in a world where healthy and connected marriages are the norm.

CONTENTS

INTRO-
DUCTION

"Hey babe, how was your day?"
"Good, how was yours?"
"It was okay. Long and pretty typical. What's for dinner?"

Does this sound familiar... same question,
same answer, different day?

Remember those dating years and how easy it was to spend hours lost in conversation? Curiosity about each other allowed time to pass so quickly. Unfortunately, the desire to get to know each other wanes as familiarity sets in, and as the years roll by, so does boredom. Finding creative ways to connect and engage with your spouse becomes an unbearable task in light of all the responsibilities weighing on us. This is where many couples find themselves: living on auto-pilot, longing for connection, but lacking resources.

THE #1 WAY TO BUILD EMOTIONAL INTIMACY IS BY ASKING OPEN-ENDED QUESTIONS

We were made for connection. How we communicate with one another is directly tied to the quality of our connection. Loneliness inside of marriage is on the rise, proving that we've lost the art of asking good questions. In this day and age, it seems like most of us are far more concerned with sharing what is on our mind than listening to others. But let's take a minute to think about what a question is. Asking a question expresses your curiosity and desire to know more. When you ask a question about your spouse's dreams, preferences, feelings, and memories it communicates that you are looking for connection.

Speaking of questions, you may ask yourself, "Will asking these questions be worth the potential awkwardness?" Well, it's only awkward because it's unfamiliar. If you haven't engaged in asking each other good questions, you will probably experience the discomfort of feeling unskilled. Embrace it! Embrace the potential awkwardness, saving yourself from years of loneliness in exchange for true connection with your spouse.

This book has the potential to turn your marriage around. Whether you binge all the questions over a weekend away, or simply ask one question a day, we are confident you will begin to see quick wins in your marriage. The conversations that will occur will create connection, which is key to a long-lasting and happy marriage.

HOW TO USE THIS BOOK

By Date

For each day of the year, there is one Connecting Question. Turn to the date of the year and take turns asking the question listed. You don't need to start on January 1! Any day is a great day to start! Simply find the date and start asking.

By Topic

If there is a specific area you want to work on in your marriage, pick a question by topic using the index (pg. 196) in the back of the book.

P.S.

We've included several blank pages (pg. 176) at the back of this book for you to write down any notes, things that might stand out to you, or things that you want to remember for the future. You can also use this book for journal prompts.

WHEN TO USE THIS BOOK

- At dinner
- In the car
- On date nights
- Over the phone
- During a weekend getaway
- On the couch after the kids go to bed
- On a coffee date
- While camping
- On a plane
- During game night
- While stranded on a deserted island
- ... Or really any time that works!

TIPS FOR MAKING THE BEST USE OF THESE QUESTIONS

Limit Distractions

Make sure you silence your phones, turn off the TV, put the kids to bed, and are ready to give 100% of your time and attention to the conversation.

Watch Your Body Language

Remember that 90% of communication is nonverbal, so be aware of tone, attitude, eye contact, and body posture. Use physical touch (hold hands, touch your husband's leg, place your hand on your wife's back) to show that you are invested in what your spouse is sharing.

Use the 'Feelings Words List' in the Back of the Book
(page 188)

Most of us use the same five emotions when we talk about experiences. It's time to expand your vocabulary! Our list will help you communicate your feelings more clearly.

Listen With Empathy

We want you to experience what a Naked Conversation is, meaning that you can share your thoughts while being vulnerable and messy, knowing that you won't be judged, minimized, fixed or ignored. Listening is a major component of connecting with your spouse. In the back of this book we offer sample phrases that express empathy as a guide for you.

Keep an Open Mind

Shocker... your spouse thinks differently than you! In order to understand each other you will need to try seeing things from your spouse's perspective. This can be frustrating if your spouse's line of reasoning defies all logic. Be prepared that your spouse might say something that will surprise you or even disappoint you. Stay away from judgement and focus your energy on listening.

Don't Interrupt

Interrupting sends a variety of messages like, "I'm more important than you," "I don't have time for your opinion," "I don't really care what you think," or "What I have to say is more interesting." If you are truly listening to understand your spouse, you will need a moment to process. It may feel uncomfortable at first, but allow space for silence, giving you both time to reflect and form your thoughts.

Watch Out for Triggers

If your marriage has been on auto-pilot for a while, some of the questions will bring up underlying issues that you have either been avoiding or minimizing. Triggers are a "warning sign" that this topic needs to be worked through. How do you know if you're triggered? Your heart starts to beat faster, your cheeks get flushed, you feel anxious, angry, frustrated, or even disapointed. Take a quick time out and go for a walk, take a shower, do some yoga, anything that will help restore a calm state before you come back to the conversation. If you can't work through it on your own, it is ok to seek counsel from a therapist to help guide you both through it.

Use "I" Statements

Try to own your feelings by using "I" statements when communicating your feelings. "I" statements are less threatening and keep the conversation calmer. For example: "I felt very confused when you shared that story," rather than "That makes no sense and it's so confusing to me."

Ask Clarifying Questions

If something your spouse shares causes confusion or they are having difficulty finding the right words, use these clarifying questions:

- How did that make you feel?
- Why do you think that is?
- Can you help me understand what you're feeling here?
- What are you most concerned about?
- Could you repeat that again?
- I want to make sure I understood you.
- Do you have mixed feelings about this?

Don't Be Too Serious

While our questions will dig deep into core memories and topics you may have been avoiding, some of the questions are just for fun and should cause some good belly laughs. Laughter and fun are two essential components of a healthy marriage.

HELP! MY SPOUSE WON'T READ THE BOOK WITH ME

Here you are. You picked up this book, came home, eagerly told your spouse about it, and you got shot down. Major mood killer! The reality is that some spouses feel threatened, anxious, and maybe even a little nervous about diving into conversations about your relationship, especially if you've been putting your relationship on the backburner. Don't let that stop you from making the most of this book.

Use the questions as journal prompts to build more self-awareness and grow more in your confidence. You can also glance at the question for the day, try your best to memorize it and casually ask it over dinner or in bed at night. Your spouse won't even know where you got the question from and they'll most likely be up for having a casual conversation with you. And whatever you do... don't stop initiating Connecting Questions with your spouse.

All marriages, no matter how good, can be made better.

1

JANUARY

JANUARY 1

Do you acknowledge and celebrate your
wins, even the small ones? How?

JANUARY 2

What three qualities about me
were you first attracted to?

JANUARY 3

Which of our past sexual experiences
have been your favorite and why?

JANUARY 4

Where can you make space in your life to
make sure you have alone time to recharge?

JANUARY 5

What would you like to be known for,
both personally and professionally?

JANUARY 6

Who are your core friends and how much time
do you think is important to spend with them?

JANUARY 7

What does it feel like when I
admit that I am wrong?

JANUARY 8

If you could change anything about the way
you were raised, what would it be and why?

JANUARY 9

What are some areas we can improve when
it comes to managing our money?

JANUARY 10

What are two things you can do
regularly to reduce stress?

JANUARY 11

If you never had to sleep, what would
you do with the extra time?

JANUARY 12

How can I show that I am
sexually attracted to you?

JANUARY 13

Do you feel like we are a team when it comes
to making decisions? Why or why not?

JANUARY 14

What roadblocks, struggles, or issues can we
not get past? What resources should
we find to help us out?

JANUARY 15

When you come home from work,
what can I do or say that will make
you feel the most loved?

JANUARY 16

If I spent a typical day in your shoes,
what would I experience?

JANUARY 17

If you could make one rule that everyone
had to follow, what would it be?

JANUARY 18

Is there anything that I commit to that is
taking time away from our marriage?

JANUARY 19

Share a time when you felt heard and understood. What emotions did you feel?

JANUARY 20

Do you prefer to have sex in the morning, the afternoon or in the evening?

JANUARY 21

In your opinion, what qualities does a healthy marriage have?

JANUARY 22

What are the characteristics of
a trustworthy person?

JANUARY 23

What is your favorite adventure
that we took together and why?

JANUARY 24

What is one financial decision you
made in the past that you regret?

JANUARY 25

Is there anything that keeps you from being
completely honest with me? Explain.

JANUARY 26

What are three of your best memories with
your family as a kid? What makes those
memories stand out to you?

JANUARY 27

How can you begin to find joy in what
you have, not in what you want?

JANUARY 28

If you could pick one year of your life to do over, which year would it be and why?

JANUARY 29

Have you ever felt alone in our marriage? Explain.

JANUARY 30

What financial legacy do you want to leave behind?

JANUARY 31

What is your secret sexual fantasy?

Great marriages don't happen by accident, but by small daily acts of intentionality.

FEBRUARY 1

What are your expectations of
how we spend Valentine's day?

FEBRUARY 2

What new tradition or ritual are you excited
about starting in our relationship?

FEBRUARY 3

How strong is your confidence
and self-worth?

FEBRUARY 4

What exactly does an orgasm feel like to you?

FEBRUARY 5

Is social media bringing us closer or
making us more isolated and alone?

FEBRUARY 6

Growing up, did you ever feel neglected
by your parents? Explain.

FEBRUARY 7

On a scale of 1-10, how connected do
you feel to me? Explain your rating.

FEBRUARY 8

What moves you and restores
your faith in humanity?

FEBRUARY 9

Is there any kind of physical touch that I can
engage in more that helps you feel loved?

FEBRUARY 10

Are there any areas where you need to forgive yourself for a mistake you have made?

FEBRUARY 11

How would you like to financially invest in our marriage? Examples: date nights, weekend getaways, go to therapy, read more marriage books, couple retreats, etc.

FEBRUARY 12

What is your favorite date that we have ever been on? What made it special to you?

FEBRUARY 13

What change could you make in your life that
would have the biggest positive impact?

FEBRUARY 14

How can we romance each other during
the day in anticipation of sex?

FEBRUARY 15

Do you feel like you can be assertive
with me? Why or why not?

FEBRUARY 16

What are three things that I do
that you could not live without?

FEBRUARY 17

Were your parents affectionate
towards each other when you were a kid?
Why do you think that was?

FEBRUARY 18

What are you most proud
of in our relationship?

FEBRUARY 19

What issue do most people think is black and white but you think has a lot of nuances?

FEBRUARY 20

Have I ever ridiculed you or made fun of your opinion or idea? How did that make you feel?

FEBRUARY 21

What does having money represent to you?

FEBRUARY 22

Do you feel like I try my best to
understand your views, feelings and opinions?
Why or why not?

FEBRUARY 23

Where are three places on your
body you like to be kissed?

FEBRUARY 24

What questions should engaged couples ask
each other before getting married?

FEBRUARY 25

Do you think you are reliable in our
relationship? Why or why not?

FEBRUARY 26

What is one thing you would like to do less of
and why? How can you make that happen?

FEBRUARY 27

What is something you did not want to do at
all that turned out to be a great experience?

FEBRUARY 28

Do you ever blame others for
your mistakes? Explain.

Communicate
your needs
even
when it's
uncomfortable.

MARCH

MARCH 1

What is your favorite way to
relax when things are hectic?

MARCH 2

What gets in the way of expressing your
expectations, feelings and needs to me?

MARCH 3

How did your parents handle
conflict when you were a kid?

MARCH 4

Is there anything you have been longing
for that might spice up our sex life?

MARCH 5

What is the best and worst thing
about getting older?

MARCH 6

What are some barriers that keep us from
apologizing when we have made a mistake?
Examples: Pride, shame, fear, doubt, rejection, etc.

MARCH 7

What compliment would you really
like to hear from me?

MARCH 8

How did your parents manage their
money when you were growing up?

MARCH 9

What is one of your guilty pleasures?

MARCH 10

How do you feel when I make you a priority?

MARCH 11

What is your moral compass for
making difficult decisions?

MARCH 12

How do you feel about sexting,
phone sex and sending each other naughty
pictures throughout the day?

MARCH 13

Which issues in our marriage
have we been avoiding?

MARCH 14

What is your earliest memory?

MARCH 15

Is there anything I have promised in the past
that I did not keep my word on?

MARCH 16

What is one failure that has turned
into your greatest lesson?

MARCH 17

What is the most meaningful thing
we have accomplished together?

MARCH 18

What is one thing that I can work on to
become a better listener?

MARCH 19

On a scale from 1-10, what is the
highest level of pain you have ever been in?
What happened?

MARCH 20

What makes you feel connected
and cared for?

MARCH 21

Who taught you about sex?
Was it helpful or a hindrance?

MARCH 22

In your opinion, what is the best way
a person can spend their time?

MARCH 23

What does self-care look like to you?
How well do you implement
self-care in your life?

MARCH 24

What amount of money would we have to earn
to make us feel financially secure?

MARCH 25

What is the most adventurous
thing you've ever done?

MARCH 26

What actions do you see that make you feel
like I do not care about our marriage? Explain.

MARCH 27

What do you wish you could tell
yourself ten years ago?

MARCH 28

Do you believe that there are some things in
life that are unforgivable? Explain.

MARCH 29

How did your parents discipline
you when you were a kid?

MARCH 30

What does our ideal sex life look like for you?

MARCH 31

If you did not have to work, what
would you do with your time?

Give your spouse your undivided attention.

APRIL

APRIL 1

What do you love about your personality?

APRIL 2

What are some of your thoughts and fears that go through your head when you are being vulnerable with your emotions?

APRIL 3

What can I do to make you feel more confident in our future together?

APRIL 4

On a scale of 1-10, how important is it
to you to be debt free? Explain.

APRIL 5

What activity in your life brings you joy?

APRIL 6

Have I done anything in the last
month that has caused you pain?
How did that make you feel?

APRIL 7

What are ways we can make our sexual
intimacy a bigger priority?

APRIL 8

Growing up, what was the
overall tone in your home?

APRIL 9

Do you think you fight fair?
Do you think I fight fair?

APRIL 10

What have you done in your life
that you are most proud of?

APRIL 11

What are two areas in your life
that you find yourself insecure about?
What is something that you can do to build
more confidence in those areas?

APRIL 12

What are the qualities of a best friend?

APRIL 13

In what ways do you consider
yourself to be unique?

APRIL 14

What would it take for you to start saying no
to things that are not as important to you so
you can say yes to the things that are?

APRIL 15

If you were given one million dollars,
what would you spend it on?

APRIL 16

What goal have you been putting off?
Why do you think that is?

APRIL 17

What are some of the highlights and
lowlights of your adolescence?

APRIL 18

How are you attracted to me physically?

APRIL 19

When you don't forgive
someone, how does it affect you?
How does it affect the other person?

APRIL 20

What is your favorite way to
spend the weekend?

APRIL 21

When was a time you felt
misunderstood by someone?

APRIL 22

What kind of legacy do you
want to leave behind?

APRIL 23

Which sex positions are your
favorite and why? Are there any
new positions you want to try?

APRIL 24

What is the primary purpose
or value of money?

APRIL 25

Do you feel like we are making enough
time for our relationship? Explain.

APRIL 26

How did you find out there was no Santa
Claus, Easter Bunny, and Tooth Fairy?

APRIL 27

To your best knowledge, how do
other people perceive you?

APRIL 28

What primary issues do we continue
to argue about? What steps do we
need to take to resolve them?

APRIL 29

Do you ever feel taken advantage
of by those you love? Explain.

APRIL 30

What was your most memorable
holiday as a kid and why?

MAY 1

What is one strange habit that most
people do not know about you?

MAY 2

What is something you always love doing,
even when you are tired or rushed and why?

MAY 3

How can I make you feel comfortable when it
comes to our physical intimacy?

MAY 4

When I spend a lot of time on my phone,
how does it make you feel?

MAY 5

What do you think will help keep
our connection to each other strong?
In what areas do you think we thrive in our marriage?
Examples: communication, sex, prioritizing
each other, having fun, etc.

MAY 6

Do you feel like a lot of the
hurts in our marriage are intentional
or unintentional? Explain.

MAY 7

How confident are you in your abilities
to make decisions for yourself?

MAY 8

How can I help you more around the house?

MAY 9

What does it look like to be financially
prepared for an emergency?

MAY 10

How do you signal to me that you are
initiating sex? Explain in detail.

MAY 11

Are you quick to apologize in
our marriage? Why or why not?

MAY 12

What was the kindest thing you
have ever done for someone?

MAY 13

What are two negative behaviors
your parents modeled?

MAY 14

What goals do you have for our family?

MAY 15

Do you tend to meet others' needs before
your own? Why or why not?

MAY 16

Have I ever done anything that made you feel like you cannot share your struggles, thoughts or ideas with me? Explain.

MAY 17

How comfortable are you with showing affection in public?

MAY 18

What characteristics do you judge the most harshly in others?

MAY 19

What is the worst piece of advice
anyone has ever given you?

MAY 20

If you were the president for one week,
what is one thing you would do?

MAY 21

Do you consider yourself a saver,
a spender or a little of both?

MAY 22

Do you struggle to trust me?
What can I do to help rebuild
trust in our marriage?

MAY 23

When was the last time you tried
something for the first time?

MAY 24

Where are you living right now –
the past, the present or the future?

MAY 25

When conflict arises, do you tend to
embrace it or avoid it? Explain.

MAY 26

Are there any feelings or thoughts that get in
the way of me giving you oral sex?

MAY 27

What memories do you have of your
family having fun together?

MAY 28

What are some of your talents?
Are you utilizing them? How can
you use them more?

MAY 29

What was your favorite part of
our wedding day?

MAY 30

If you could talk to your teenage self,
what would you say?

MAY 31

What areas of our marriage do we need to talk about, even if it is uncomfortable?

Loving well
requires
listening
well.

JUNE

JUNE 1

What are some activities and adventures
you want to plan for the summer?

JUNE 2

What is the best financial decision
you made in the past?

JUNE 3

Have my words or actions ever made
you feel insecure? Explain.

JUNE 4

Growing up, did you ever feel like you could
not show emotion? Explain.

JUNE 5

Which ten words would you
use to describe yourself?

JUNE 6

On the days we do not have much time for
physical intimacy, what are some ways that I
can help you get in the mood quicker?

JUNE 7

What time of the day is the best time for us
to have heart-to-heart conversations?

JUNE 8

What are some healthy boundaries you
have put in place in your life?

JUNE 9

In what ways do painful experiences
help us grow as a couple?

JUNE 10

When are you the most inspired, most
motivated, and most charged up?

JUNE 11

What passion do we share that
we can pursue together?

JUNE 12

What is your biggest struggle when
communicating? What is one thing you can
do today to start working on that?

JUNE 13

What are you doing currently
to better yourself?

JUNE 14

What are two positive patterns and/or beliefs
that your parents taught you as a child?

JUNE 15

What do you enjoy about our sex life?

JUNE 16

When was the most difficult time of your
life and how has that affected you?

JUNE 17

What is the most memorable
gift you ever received?

JUNE 18

When did you know you were in love with me?

JUNE 19

If we ran a business together,
what would it be?

JUNE 20

What would you like to
change about yourself?

JUNE 21

What are some ways that the internet and
social media have changed the way people
communicate with each other?

JUNE 22

What is one area that I can work on when it
comes to money and our marriage?

JUNE 23

Growing up, were you ever left out,
bullied or made fun of by your peers
or family members? Explain.

JUNE 24

How do you feel about the pace of your life?
Is it too fast, too slow, or just about right?

JUNE 25

What do you have to say no to in order to
accomplish your goals and desires?

JUNE 26

Do you feel anxious about any specific
body part of yours or mine?

JUNE 27

Is there anything I need to apologize for that
has chipped away at your trust of me?

JUNE 28

What are some of your dreams
and desires for your life?

JUNE 29

What are your thoughts about
marriage counseling? Do you think
there have been times where it would
have helped our marriage?

JUNE 30

How often do you prefer to spend
quality time together?

Happily Ever
After isn't a
fairytale,
it's a choice.

JULY 7

JULY 1

What is our number one financial
priority this month?

JULY 2

What triggers you during conflict?
Examples: cussing, name calling, the silent
treatment, defensiveness, eye rolling, etc.

JULY 3

As a couple, how can we give back
to others or to our community in a way
that we are not currently doing?

JULY 4

Is there anything you would like
to me start doing to you sexually that
I have not been doing?

JULY 5

How did we make each other smile this week?

JULY 6

Do you think actions speak louder than
words? Why or why not?

JULY 7

Have you ever upset someone because of a
boundary you put into place? What happened?

JULY 8

On a scale of 1-10 (10 = excellent, 1 = closed
off), how vulnerable are we in our heart-to-
heart communication? Explain your rating.

JULY 9

Have you spent time reflecting
on your past to help you understand
who you are today? Explain.

JULY 10

What characteristics do you judge
the most harshly in yourself?

JULY 11

What does being financially
comfortable look like to you?

JULY 12

Why do you think pornography use is on the
rise with both men and women? In what way
do you think it presents a false fantasy?

JULY 13

What can I do that provides the greatest
comfort and encouragement to you when you
are hurt, fearful, anxious, or worried?

JULY 14

Who is a great example of forgiveness,
both historical and in your own life?

JULY 15

What kinds of gifts do you
prefer for me to buy you for your
birthday and our anniversary?

JULY 16

How are we similar and are our similarities
a good thing for our marriage?

JULY 17

Do we effectively communicate about areas
of conflict in our marriage? Explain.

JULY 18

What was your bedroom like as a teenager?

JULY 19

How soon after an argument
are you willing to be intimate?
What are your thoughts about "makeup sex"?

JULY 20

What are you most grateful for in life?

JULY 21

How did your parents soothe
you when you were a kid?

JULY 22

How would you describe our
communication style?

JULY 23

When we work together on our budget and
financial goals, how does it make you feel?

JULY 24

What topics do we deal with as a couple that we will not
discuss with our parents and family members?
Examples: Our parenting, our sex life, our
money, our careers, our arguments. etc.

JULY 25

Who are the five people you
spend the most time with?

JULY 26

What kind of legacy do you want
our marriage to reflect?

JULY 27

How do you like to be kissed?

JULY 28

How would you like to grow
when faced with conflict?

JULY 29

Who is the first person that comes to mind
if you were asked about the greatest hurt in
your life? What thoughts or triggers come up
when you think about that person?

JULY 30

If you could trade places with any person
right now, who would it be and why?

JULY 31

What is something you are
self-conscious about?

Don't give up!
Great
marriages
Take Time.

AUGUST

AUGUST 1

What are three things that are
or should be on your bucket list?

AUGUST 2

How do our differences complement us?

AUGUST 3

Are you comfortable with your
body and with being naked?

AUGUST 4

Do you feel that respect and trust have
to be earned? Why or why not?

AUGUST 5

How can we make sure that divorce
is NEVER an option for us?

AUGUST 6

Who was your childhood hero and why?

AUGUST 7

What do you think happens after death?

AUGUST 8

How much money can each of us
spend per month without any rules and
without having to ask permission?

AUGUST 9

What is something you have always
felt was missing from your life?

AUGUST 10

When do you need assurance
of my love the most?

AUGUST 11

If we eliminated physical attraction from our
relationship, what would be left?

AUGUST 12

How or when do you feel most
connected with God?

AUGUST 13

What is the most embarrassing
moment of your life?

AUGUST 14

How do you think we could
have more fun together?

AUGUST 15

What are some qualities of a good listener?

AUGUST 16

In your opinion, which characteristics
make someone reliable?

AUGUST 17

When someone chooses not to forgive the
person who caused them pain, what do you
think will happen over time?

AUGUST 18

When I am angry, how can I clearly
communicate my position without
becoming defensive or attacking?

AUGUST 19

What boundaries can we put in place
that will protect us from spending too
much time on our phones?

AUGUST 20

Who do you look up to as an example
of a healthy marriage?

AUGUST 21

When I compliment you, how
does it make you feel?

AUGUST 22

Are there any charitable foundations you
would like to give to financially?

AUGUST 23

What habits or addictions have been passed down from
previous generations? How has that impacted your life?
Examples: alcoholism, mental illness, addictions,
divorce, adultery, etc.

AUGUST 24

How does it make you feel when
you bring me to orgasm?

AUGUST 25

Do you struggle with comparison?
Who do you compare yourself to and how
does that impact you?

AUGUST 26

Do you feel like you are realistic with your
expectations of me? Why or why not?

AUGUST 27

What does it feel like when I give
you a sincere apology?

AUGUST 28

What did you want to be when
you were a kid and why?

AUGUST 29

Do you feel like you have control over your
emotions most of the time? Why or why not?

AUGUST 30

What did you learn from watching
your parents handle money?

AUGUST 31

Have you ever felt like one or both of us avoids sensitive topics? Why or why not?

Never stop showing your spouse how much you love them.

SEPTEMBER

SEPTEMBER 1

How can we grow in our marriage? Be specific.

SEPTEMBER 2

Did you grow up feeling validated by
your parents and siblings? Explain.

SEPTEMBER 3

Which of our friends do you like
spending time with and why?

SEPTEMBER 4

What would you like to accomplish together?

SEPTEMBER 5

Which area of your life is in the most
need of healthy boundaries?

SEPTEMBER 6

What would you do with five million dollars
to impact the most amount of people?

SEPTEMBER 7

How can I show you sexually
how much I love you?

SEPTEMBER 8

What qualities do you consider a person
with spiritual peace to have?

SEPTEMBER 9

What are external factors that have
gotten in our way of communicating?
Examples: TV is always on, noisy kids, phone
alerts, bringing work home, etc.

SEPTEMBER 10

Have you ever been jealous of someone or
something in my life? Tell me about it.

SEPTEMBER 11

How and when will we resolve the
differences in our marriage?

SEPTEMBER 12

What is your favorite part of our foreplay?
Is there anything different you would like to try?

SEPTEMBER 13

How would you spend your time if the
electricity went out for 24 hours?

SEPTEMBER 14

When you are ill, how much sympathy and
attention do you desire from me?

SEPTEMBER 15

What was your favorite part
of our honeymoon?

SEPTEMBER 16

Do we tend to fight about the
same things over and over again?
Why do you think that is?

SEPTEMBER 17

At what age do you want to retire
and what type of lifestyle do you want
to lead in retirement?

SEPTEMBER 18

When your parents got angry, either with each
other or with you, how did it make you feel?

SEPTEMBER 19

How important is celebrating our anniversary, your birthday, and holidays to you?

SEPTEMBER 20

If we made a movie together, what would the title be and who would play us?

SEPTEMBER 21

Do either of us make excuses to not have sex? Explain.

SEPTEMBER 22

When you approach a conversation
with me, do you ever feel nervous
or anxious? Why or why not?

SEPTEMBER 23

Have you ever set an unrealistic goal?
What happened?

SEPTEMBER 24

Which people seem to consistently break trust
in your life? What can you do about it?

SEPTEMBER 25

Do you feel like we have enough
heart-to-heart conversations that
connect us emotionally? What does it feel
like to be emotionally connected?

SEPTEMBER 26

What specific areas in our relationship
are we lacking trust in?

SEPTEMBER 27

When do you feel most connected to me?

SEPTEMBER 28

What is the difference between
failing and being a failure?

SEPTEMBER 29

How would you like to be held before,
during, and after sex?

SEPTEMBER 30

What stresses you out when
talking about money?

Your spouse needs to know that you're on the same team, fighting for them, not against them.

OCTOBER

10

OCTOBER 1

When you feel alone in our marriage,
what are your go to's to help numb the pain?
Examples: TV, alcohol, reading, eating, porn,
shopping, video games, etc.

OCTOBER 2

What is one small change you
can make this week that will help you
feel in control of your life?

OCTOBER 3

Do you want to work part-time, full-time,
or be a stay-at-home mom/dad?

OCTOBER 4

In what way(s) has our
relationship changed you?

OCTOBER 5

How often would you like to have sex?

OCTOBER 6

How would you feel if your life
and our marriage looked exactly the
same in five years?

OCTOBER 7

What are boundaries that we need
to set up to protect ourselves from
unhealthy family members and friends?

OCTOBER 8

What are some unhealthy habits
that we have when we communicate?
Examples: Name calling, blaming, fixing, minimizing
feelings, making judgmental statements, eye rolling,
shutting down, etc.

OCTOBER 9

When in your life have you hurt others close
to you? Have you apologized?

OCTOBER 10

What is your idea of the perfect date night?

OCTOBER 11

When you face challenges,
do you feel overwhelmed and hopeless
or empowered and excited?

OCTOBER 12

What is the most erotic thing I
can do in the bedroom?

OCTOBER 13

What beliefs do you have about yourself
that resulted from your childhood?

OCTOBER 14

How does it feel when I communicate to
you and show a lot of emotion?

OCTOBER 15

What is your most selfish
character trait or habit?

OCTOBER 16

What are three things that bore you?

OCTOBER 17

How does it make you feel when I address
conflict in our relationship?

OCTOBER 18

What are three practical ways that
I can show my love for you?

OCTOBER 19

What makes you angry and what do you
do when you are really angry?

OCTOBER 20

What one thing do you really want
to purchase but can't afford?

OCTOBER 21

Are you comfortable discussing our sexual
likes and dislikes? Why or why not?

OCTOBER 22

How would you rate your childhood growing
up on a scale of 1-10 (10 = amazing and 1 =
terrible)? Why did you give that score?
Be specific with your reasoning.

OCTOBER 23

What makes you feel the most insecure?
How do you handle your insecurities?

OCTOBER 24

Are you someone who can say no and draw
boundaries even when it makes others angry
or uncomfortable? Why or why not?

OCTOBER 25

When it comes to sex, do you like
it when I am in control or do you
prefer to take the lead?

OCTOBER 26

How do you deal with disappointments?

OCTOBER 27

In your view, what should the husband's
role in a marriage be?

OCTOBER 28

In your view, what should the
wife's role in a marriage be?

OCTOBER 29

What is something adventurous you have
always wanted to experience?

OCTOBER 30

When was a time in your life where trust was
broken and it made a big impact on you?

OCTOBER 31

If you could spend a day talking to one person,
alive or dead, who would it be and why?

The best gift you can give your spouse is your TIME.

NOVEMBER

NOVEMBER 1

Growing up, how did the holiday season make
you feel? Was it chaotic or happy?

NOVEMBER 2

How do you feel about scheduling sex?

NOVEMBER 3

Which do you think should have the final say
in decision making: logic or emotions? Why?

NOVEMBER 4

Do you ever struggle with
communicating your needs in our
relationship? Why or why not?

NOVEMBER 5

Is there any argument that we had this past
month that you feel is unresolved?

NOVEMBER 6

Based on our marriage experiences, what
advice would you give people who are dating?

NOVEMBER 7

What is a new holiday tradition
you want to start this year?

NOVEMBER 8

What role does gratitude play in your life?

NOVEMBER 9

Are there any people in our lives that gossip
about others often? How can we protect our
marriage from this person?

NOVEMBER 10

Growing up, what were your favorite
Thanksgiving traditions?

NOVEMBER 11

What are your biggest worries
about the future?

NOVEMBER 12

What could I say and do to make
you feel more respected?

NOVEMBER 13

Is connecting emotionally before
we have sex important to you?
If so, how would you like to connect?

NOVEMBER 14

When you are going through a difficult
time, who can you go to that will give
you objective feedback to help you process
what you are going through?

NOVEMBER 15

What are you most excited
for this holiday season?

NOVEMBER 16

Were you allowed to express your
emotions as a kid? Why or why not?

NOVEMBER 17

What budget do we need to put in place for
spending money on presents for us and our
family members during this holiday season?

NOVEMBER 18

If you could get away with a crime,
would you? If yes, what would it be?

NOVEMBER 19

Why do you believe some people get stuck in their ways and never change their behaviors?

NOVEMBER 20

How would you like to give to others this holiday season?

NOVEMBER 21

If you could spend your next week anywhere in the world, where would you go?

NOVEMBER 22

When did you laugh harder than
any other time in your life?

NOVEMBER 23

What makes our relationship special?

NOVEMBER 24

What is the difference between a
sincere and an insincere apology?

NOVEMBER 25

Growing up, what were your
favorite Christmas traditions?

NOVEMBER 26

If you had a choice, which era
would you choose to live in?

NOVEMBER 27

Where are three places you would like to
make love other than on our bed?

NOVEMBER 28

How do you feel about your current
relationship with your parents?

NOVEMBER 29

Do you feel like we are good stewards
of what we have been given?

NOVEMBER 30

Do you feel like I validate or dismiss
your opinions? Explain.

If you want to make a better marriage, make a better you.

12

DECEMBER

DECEMBER 1

What stresses you out most about the holiday season?
Examples: crowded stores, seeing relatives, spending
money, too many holiday parties, pressures at work,
being around a lot of alcohol, etc.

DECEMBER 2

Do you feel comfortable asking for help
from me when you feel unsure of something?
Why or why not?

DECEMBER 3

What causes and movements
are you passionate about?

DECEMBER 4

What would you like more of in our marriage?

DECEMBER 5

Is there anything that makes you feel uncomfortable about my parents and family?

DECEMBER 6

What do we need to say no to so we can make sure we are spending quality time together this holiday season?

DECEMBER 7

When was the last time you cried?
What did you cry about?

DECEMBER 8

In what areas do you find it the
hardest to be open and honest with me?
Why do you think that is?

DECEMBER 9

What areas in our life have
gotten in the way of making our
physical intimacy a priority?

DECEMBER 10

How does prayer play a role in your day?

DECEMBER 11

If you could be insanely talented at one
thing, what would you choose?

DECEMBER 12

What has taken up too much of
your energy in life?

DECEMBER 13

How did your parents show their love for you?

DECEMBER 14

Do you feel like we have a good understanding
of how and when we should bring up issues in
our marriage? Why or why not?

DECEMBER 15

What goal would you like to concentrate
on before the year is up?

DECEMBER 16

Do you feel like I minimize your fears,
concerns or desires with my words
or actions? Explain.

DECEMBER 17

What five things would you pick to take with
you if you were on a deserted island?

DECEMBER 18

Have any of your friendships become
strained or distant over time?
Why do you think that is?

DECEMBER 19

What would your dream house be like
and what city would it be in?

DECEMBER 20

How can we verbally express satisfaction
during foreplay and sex?

DECEMBER 21

What does it mean to be trustworthy?

DECEMBER 22

Do you feel like you can identify and
communicate your feelings to me?
Why or why not?

DECEMBER 23

What things in your life do you feel
like you have not let go of that keep
you from true happiness?

DECEMBER 24

Which book has had the greatest
impact on your life?

DECEMBER 25

What is the best Christmas
gift you ever received?

DECEMBER 26

What are the greatest challenges
to healthy communication?

DECEMBER 27

What areas have we been putting
in front of our marriage?
Examples: kids, work, friends, social media,
family, hobbies, technology, etc.

DECEMBER 28

Do you believe in second chances?
Why or why not?

DECEMBER 29

What is one bad habit you need to break,
but do not want to?

DECEMBER 30

What do you hope for in the
next year of our marriage?

DECEMBER 31

If you died tomorrow, what legacy
would you leave in the world?

NOTES

....

....

....

....

....

....

....

....

....

....

....

....

....

....

....

....

....

....

....

....

....

....

....

....

....

....

....

....

....

....

....

....

....

....

....

....

FEELINGS
WORDS LIST

USE THIS LIST TO HELP YOU COMMUNICATE YOUR FEELINGS MORE CLEARLY

loved - romantic - appreciative - refreshed - comforted

peaceful - relieved - comforted - relaxed - protected

confident - secure - positive - assertive - self-assured

happy - elated - joyful - satisfied - optimistic - delighted

excited - playful - determined - talkative - rejuvenated

ashamed - guilty - embarrassed - stupid - exposed

sad - hopeless - unhappy - crushed - desperate

anxious - uneasy - worried - fearful - indecisive

alone - abandoned - isolated - disconnected

angry - controlled - grumpy - irritated - bitter

confused - misunderstood - deceived - skeptical

exhausted - depressed - withdrawn - lazy - beaten down

overwhelmed - burdened - guarded - tense - confused

You can change
your marriage
by changing
your attitude.

PHRASES
THAT
EXPRESS
EMPATHY

I understand how you're feeling.

How disappointing.

This makes sense.

You must feel so helpless.

I'm on your team, babe.

That would hurt my feelings too.

Tell me more.

I agree 100%.

I think you're right.

That would make me mad too.

I'm on your side here.

So what you're saying is...

True love is selfless.

INDEX

BOUNDARIES

Jan 4, 18 // Feb 5, 26 // Mar 10, 23 // Apr 14, 25, 29 // May 4, 15 // Jun 8, 25 // Jul 7, 24 // Aug 19 // Sep 5, 24 // Oct 7, 24 // Nov 9 // Dec 5, 6, 12, 27

CHILDHOOD

Jan 8, 26 // Feb 6, 17 // Mar 3, 14, 29 // Apr 8, 17, 30 // May 13, 27 // Jun 4, 14, 23 // Jul 9, 18 // Aug 6, 23, 28 // Sep 2, 18 // Oct 13, 22 // Nov 10, 16, 25 // Dec 13

COMMUNICATION

Jan 19, 25 // Feb 15, 22 // Mar 2, 18 // Apr 2, 21 // May 16, 31 // Jun 7, 12, 21 // Jul 8, 17, 22 // Aug 15, 18, 26 // Sep 9, 22, 25 // Oct 8, 14 // Nov 4, 30 // Dec 2, 8, 16, 22, 26

CONFLICT

Jan 14, 29 // Feb 20, 28 // Mar 13, 26 // Apr 9, 28 // May 6, 25 // Jun 3, 29 // Jul 2, 28 // Aug 5, 18 // Sep 16 // Oct 1, 17 // Nov 30 // Dec 14

FRIENDSHIP

Jan 2, 13, 15, 23 // **Feb** 2, 7, 12, 18 // **Mar** 7, 17, 20 // **Apr** 3, 12, 25 // **May** 5, 8, 14, 29 // **Jun** 11, 18, 30 // **Jul** 5, 13, 15, 26 // **Aug** 2, 10, 14 // **Sep** 1, 4, 15, 27 // **Oct** 4, 10, 18 // **Nov** 12, 23 // **Dec** 4, 30

HOLIDAYS

Feb 1 // **Apr** 30 // **Sep** 19 // **Nov** 1, 7, 15, 17, 20, 25 // **Dec** 1, 6, 15, 25

JUST FOR FUN

Jan 11, 17, 28 // **Feb** 16, 27 // **Mar** 9, 25, 31 // **Apr** 13, 20, 26 // **May** 1, 19, 20, 23 // **Jun** 1, 17, 19 // **Jul** 18, 30 // **Aug** 1, 9, 13, 28 // **Sep** 13, 20 // **Oct** 16, 29, 31 // **Nov** 18, 21, 22, 26 // **Dec** 11, 17, 19, 24, 28

MONEY

Jan 9, 24, 30 // **Feb** 11, 21 // **Mar** 8, 24 // **Apr** 4, 15, 24 // **May** 9, 21 // **Jun** 2, 22 // **Jul** 1, 11, 23 // **Aug** 8, 22, 30 // **Sep** 6, 17, 30 // **Oct** 3, 20 // **Nov** 8, 17, 29

REPAIR

Jan 7, 22 // **Feb** 10, 25 // **Mar** 6, 15, 28 // **Apr** 6, 19 // **May** 11, 22 // **Jun** 9, 27 // **Jul** 14, 29 // **Aug** 4, 17, 27 // **Sep** 11, 26 // **Oct** 9, 30 // **Nov** 5, 24 // **Dec** 21, 23

SELF-AWARENESS

Jan 1, 6, 5, 10, 16, 21, 27 // **Feb** 3, 8, 10, 13, 19, 24 // **Mar** 1, 5, 11, 16, 19, 22, 27 // **Apr** 1, 5, 10, 11, 12, 16, 22, 27 // **May** 2, 7, 12, 18, 24, 28, 30 // **Jun** 5, 10, 13, 16, 20, 24, 28 // **Jul** 3, 6, 9, 10, 16, 20, 25, 31 // **Aug** 2, 7, 12, 16, 20, 25, 29 // **Sep** 3, 8, 10, 14, 19, 23, 28 // **Oct** 2, 6, 11, 15, 19, 23, 26, 27, 28 // **Nov** 3, 6, 11, 14, 19, 28 // **Dec** 3, 7, 10, 12, 18, 29, 31

SEX AND INTIMACY

Jan 3, 12, 20, 31 // **Feb** 4, 9, 14, 23 // **Mar** 4, 12, 21, 30 // **Apr** 7, 18, 23 // **May** 3, 10, 17, 26 // **Jun** 6, 15, 26 // **Jul** 4, 12, 19, 27 // **Aug** 3, 11, 24 // **Sep** 7, 12, 21, 29 // **Oct** 5, 12, 21, 25 // **Nov** 2, 13, 27 // **Dec** 9, 20

Create a safe place for your spouse to share their dreams, ideas and concerns.

ABOUT
MARRIAGE365

Known as the couple least likely to succeed, Casey and Meygan faced every obstacle imaginable on the way to their happily ever after. After turning things around, they began sharing relationship and marriage tips on social media in 2013 and quickly realized that they weren't alone and that there was a demand for their resources. Millions of couples are trying to figure out this thing called marriage, so Casey and Meygan decided to do something about it.

They co-founded Marriage365 later that year and have since created a variety of resources and programs for couples in every stage of their relationship. From seriously dating and newlyweds to relationships in crisis, Marriage365 provides couples practical tools and a safe place to grow and learn how to be a better partner.

Marriage365 is a 501(c)(3) non-profit reaching millions of couples each month around the world. Our mission is that one day, the world will be transformed through communities made healthy because connected married couples are the norm.

You can follow us on social media @marriage365 or visit us on the web at marriage365.org.

If you like this book, make sure to check our other titles in this series:

For Engaged Couples

For Families

To purchase a copy, go to marriage365.org/store